What to doodle?

AT THE ZOO

Jillian Phillips

Dover Publications, Inc.
Mineola, New York

Bibliographical Note

What to Doodle? At the Zoo is a new work, first published by
Dover Publications, Inc., in 2010.

International Standard Book Number

ISBN-13: 978-0-486-47818-0
ISBN-10: 0-486-47818-1

Manufactured in the United States by LSC Communications
47818107   2020
www.doverpublications.com

Note

Where can you find a giraffe, a crocodile, a lemur, and a cuddly koala, all in one place—at the zoo! This little book is filled with drawings of zoo animals that you can complete yourself. Just add your own finishing touches to the pages—such as an igloo for the penguins and a den for the wolf—and you'll see why a zoo is such an interesting and fun place to visit.

What's missing on the mommy giraffe?

Giraffes have really long necks to reach the leaves at the top of the tree. Can you draw this giraffe's really long neck?

What is the panda eating?

What do a panda's eyes look like?

Where are the crocodile's teeth?
Draw them!

open wide!

What patterns would look nice on these crocodiles?

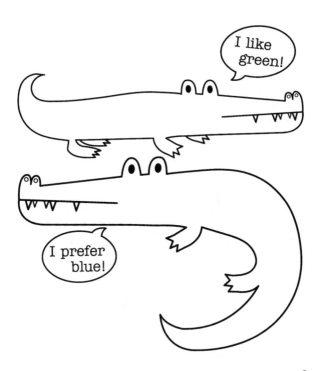

Can you draw an igloo for these penguins?

What does a lion's mouth look like?

Can you draw the lion's mane?

What do the spots look like
on this baby leopard?

What is this mommy leopard
looking for?

What does a monkey's face look like?

Who is swinging from the tree?

How many horns does a rhino have?

18

The rhino wants to find a place to
cool off from the sun. Can you
draw him a pond to get some water?

What do a walrus's teeth look like?

What does the baby walrus need so she can swim?

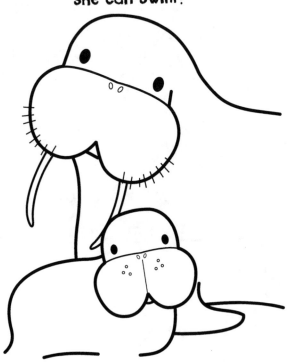

What patterns do the zebras have?

What do zebras like to eat?

What is the polar bear standing on?

What can the polar bear see
in the water?

Can you draw a hippo's face?

Where does the hippo like to
take a bath?

What is the seal looking at over the rocks?

What is the seal playing with?

What's at the end of the rattlesnake's tail?

What patterns can you give
these snakes?

The gorilla likes to play in the trees.
Can you draw some more?

What is on the ground for him to eat?

What do the elephants need to take a bath?

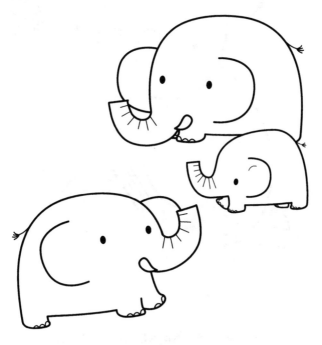

Draw it on these pages.

How does the koala hold on
to the tree?

What does a koala's nose look like?

What kind of tail does the
Red Panda have?

Draw a friend for the Red Panda.

What are these meerkats looking at?

Who is in the kangaroo's pouch?

What is the kangaroo
jumping over?

What kind of legs do flamingos have?

Where is the flamingo standing?

What is the toucan sitting on?

What kind of beak does the
toucan have?

What is missing from the tiger's fur?

What do a tiger's teeth look like?

What kind of eyes does an owl have?

Owls are always up at night.
What is in the sky above the owl?

How many humps does a camel have?

Can you draw some sand for the camels?

Can you draw a tortoise shell?

What patterns would look good on
these tortoises?

Where will this wolf go to sleep?

What is the wolf dreaming about?

How many legs does a tarantula have?

Can you help design this spider's web?

What kind of tail does this lemur have?

Can you draw a snack for the lemur family?

It's feeding time at the zoo!
Who's hungry?

What is the buffalo grazing on?